For Lesley.

Here's hoping you'll leave ... think you'll get ... inspires you to come and ... the ... and ... visited Carluke ... 60 civilised ... some great pubs too!

Richard x

The Listeners

Richard Swan

authorHOUSE®

AuthorHouse™ UK Ltd.
500 Avebury Boulevard
Central Milton Keynes, MK9 2BE
www.authorhouse.co.uk
Phone: 08001974150

First published by AuthorHouse 4/6/2009

ISBN: 978-1-4389-6224-5 (sc)

Printed in the United States of America
Bloomington, Indiana

This book is printed on acid-free paper.

Contents

Dedications page

Thank you to my 3 Princesses

Joanna, Erin Rose and Cara Jane

for helping me find my own Listener

Thank you Anne for your artistic flair

with the illustrations

Thank you Jim for your photographic skills

Thank you for sharing the wisdom:

Eckhart Tolle

Deepak Chopra

Brian Tracy

Bruce Muzik

Tale 1 - Erin and her lost Tigger

Erin was sad.

She was in her bedroom, lying on her bed with her face in the pillow, crying.

Erin was a lovely little 4-year-old girl with beautiful curly hair and she was normally very happy and smiley. But she had lost her favourite cuddly toy and it had made her very sad indeed.

'What's wrong?' said a voice in the room

'I can't find Tigger.' cried Erin without looking up

'Yes you can,' said the soft, calm voice

'No I can't!' shouted Erin into the pillow, 'I've looked and looked, and I can't find Tigger!' she cried as streams of tears flowed down her cheeks and onto the soaking wet pillow.

'Yes you can, you know where Tigger is,' assured the voice

'No, I can't Mum! I can't!' Erin cried louder

'I'm not your mum.' whispered the voice

'Well I still can't find it Dad!' screamed Erin

'I'm not your dad either.' said the voice

Erin suddenly stopped crying. She almost stopped breathing. When she had heard the voice to begin with, she just assumed it had been her mum that had come into the room to calm her down.

If the voice wasn't her mum and wasn't her dad - who was it? Very slowly and very silently Erin lifted her head up off the pillow and turned her body so that she could look around the room.

There was no one there.

A lot of her toys were lying on the floor, scattered everywhere from when she had looked for her lost Tigger. Her clothes were lying in a nice pile on top of her chest of drawers, where her mum had left them after doing the ironing. Her fairy lights were switched on around her door and her new make-up-doll's head was also sitting on top of her little desk. But there was no one else in the room.

Her tears had stopped running. Her breathing was very slow and quiet. Who on earth had been speaking? Very quietly, Erin whispered,

'Hello?'

There was silence and after a few seconds Erin relaxed and started to take a deep breath again. But as she did, the mysterious voice returned.

'Hello Erin,' it said softly and in a nice friendly tone

Erin couldn't believe it. There was no one to be seen. But she heard the voice very clearly as if someone was standing right in front of her.

'Hello?' she whispered again

This time the voice replied right away, 'Hello again Erin,' it said happily

'Who are you?' whispered Erin as her big brown eyes darted all round the room looking for where the voice was coming from.

'I'm here to help,' it said

Erin opened her wardrobe door quickly to try and catch the voice.

Only her nice dresses and shoes were there.

'But who are you?' she asked

'I'm a Listener,' whispered the voice 'and I'm here to help you find Tigger.'

'But I've looked for hours and hours,' pleaded Erin 'and can't find him anywhere.' she said, remembering how sad and upset she had been at losing her favourite cuddly toy.

Erin didn't know who the voice was but she wasn't scared. It was a nice voice; a soft voice. She kept looking for it, opening drawers and looking under her bed, but she was now more interested in getting help to find Tigger than wondering where the voice was coming from.

The voice gave a little chuckle. 'You haven't been looking for hours and hours; it's actually only been 10 minutes.' it said with a little laugh.

'Well it's felt like hours,' appealed Erin. 'How are you going to help me anyway?' she asked.

'Because I can help you remember where you've put Tigger,' it said softly.

'Rubbish! I don't know where Tigger is. If I could remember, then I'd find him!' demanded Erin.

'Yes you do.' the voice said, 'you know exactly where Tigger is'

'NO I DON'T!' shouted Erin. She was starting to get angry now. Who was this voice and why was it not helping her find Tigger when it had said it would.

'You do know where Tigger is, but you will only remember if you calm down.' appealed the voice.

Erin was still quite angry; she shouted 'And just how am I supposed to calm down?'

There was silence.

'WELL THEN?' Erin shouted again at the empty room.

Still silence.

Erin realised that the voice was not going to talk to her until she had calmed down. She huffed a bit, shrugged her shoulders, then sighed a bit more, and slowly she started to calm down.

'That's better,' the voice suddenly spoke again; 'now I want you to calm down even more and I'll help you remember.' it said.

'How do I do that?' Erin asked. She was even calmer now and wasn't shouting anymore.

'I want you to put your two hands on your tummy, just under your belly button,' it said.

'What? How's that going to help me calm down?' Erin shouted.

There was silence

'Oh, fine then. There!' she huffed and moaned as she rested her two hands on her tummy.

'Excellent,' the voice said, 'now I want you to breathe, but I want you to do it in a special way,' it said slowly. 'I want you to take a big, long, deep breath in. And when you do, you should feel your tummy filling up with air and pushing out against your hands. Not your chest, your tummy.'

Erin took a big deep breath but she never felt her tummy move. All the air had just gone into her chest. So she tried again. She took another deep breath and another, and this time she felt her tummy fill up just a little bit. So she concentrated harder and bit-by-bit she started to get the hang of it. She started to feel it working. Now every deep breath was going right down into her tummy and pushing her two hands out.

'That's it,' said the voice, 'you've got it! Keep doing that but make your breaths even longer and even slower.' it whispered.

Erin took long, slow, deep breaths and kept concentrating on how her tummy was moving out when she breathed in, and then she would puff the air out of her mouth slowly. She found that she could do it better and easier if she breathed in through her nose and then let the air out through her mouth. She was concentrating so much that she had completely forgot where she was, and didn't notice that the voice had stopped talking.

It then spoke again. 'That's perfect,' it said, 'now I want you to keep breathing and close your eyes. I'm a Listener and I'm going to help you find Tigger.'

Erin closed her eyes and kept breathing slowly without saying a word.

'Now I want you to think back to when you were playing in your room this morning and I want you to picture it inside your head,' whispered the secret voice. 'You've got a great imagination and I want you to see the pictures in your mind of how you were playing on your bedroom floor this morning with your shop till.' said the voice

Erin could remember that. She had been sitting on her floor with her little toy till, the silver coins, the vegetables and the tins and she had been playing shop. She could see it all inside her mind as she thought back. She could remember all the colours of the tins; she could see what clothes she had been wearing. And there was Tigger!

'That's right!' Erin thought, 'Tigger had been the customer in my shop and I was pretending to sell the food to him.'

She was excited and stopped breathing slowly and almost lost the picture from her mind. She quickly calmed herself down again, started her long, slow breathing again, and the picture returned. There was Tigger sitting on the floor beside her; now what had happened next? She thought and thought. Then she remembered that her mum had shouted upstairs and asked her to bring down her pirate costume, so that her mum could iron it for her to wear in the Gala Day procession at the weekend.

Erin kept her breaths nice and slow and she could remember everything that had happened in the morning. She saw herself push the toyshop stuff away under her bed. Then she had lifted up Tigger and went to her costume box.

'What had happened, what had happened?' she thought.

Then she remembered how she had lifted her pirate costume out of the box.

'Yes! That's what I did!' she thought to herself, 'I had put Tigger into the box and asked him to watch it while I took the pirate costume down to Mum!'

It had all come back to her. When she had taken the costume downstairs, her mum had given Erin her lunch and then they had went to nursery school. She had forgotten all about Tigger because she had been so busy. Erin quickly opened her eyes wide and ran to the corner of her room where her costume box was sitting. She was so excited. She lifted up the lid and threw it on her bed.

There he was! Right at the top of the box, on top of all her costumes, Tigger was sitting there just waiting to be found.

'Tigger!' Erin screamed with joy. She grabbed him up and gave him a great big hug; it was so great to have him back. Erin then ran out of her room and downstairs to tell her mum that she had found Tigger.

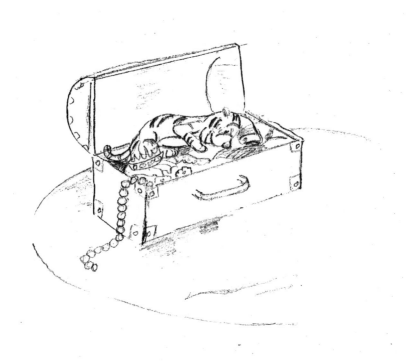

Tale 2 – Cian and Grandpa

Cian was confused.

He stood in the middle of the living room looking round at all the sad faces of the people that were there. Cian was nearly five years old now but he still didn't like wearing the tie that his mum had made him put on that morning. He felt it itchy on his neck and he was tugging and pulling at it, as he looked all around him.

All the men there were also wearing ties, black ties. There was Uncle Jack and Dad and Uncle Tommy. They were all dressed in black suits with white shirts and black ties; they all looked the same. All their sad faces also looked the same. His dad and Uncle Tommy were normally so happy and were always playing with Cian and having fun, but now they were very serious and talking quietly with other adults.

'Ah, and there's Jim's favourite grandson,' said one of the men standing in the room, as he reached down and ruffled Cian's hair.

Cian didn't like when adults did that to him. He pulled away and walked through to the kitchen.

There was Mum beside the cooker with Aunty Mary, who was taking out a big tray of sausage rolls. Cian had never seen so much food; there were trays and trays of sandwiches, sausage rolls, cakes and biscuits in every room of the house. All the people were nibbling on the food and talking quietly to each other. He watched his Aunty Mary carefully carry the tray and he could see that her eyes were still all red and puffy; he had saw her crying really hard when they had all left that big stone building this morning.

'Hello darling,' said his mum when she spotted him. She knelt down and gave him a big hug; she seemed to be hugging him a lot today but he didn't mind, as it was really nice.

'Are you ok?' she asked

'Fine,' said Cian

'That's my big brave soldier. Go and take this tray of biscuits through to the den please,' she asked him.

That had been the hundredth time that his mum had called him a brave soldier today; he didn't understand. The first time she had said it was when they both walked into the big stone building past the rows and rows of people that had all been sitting there waiting on them. Cian had been walking along quite happily, holding his mum's hand and looking at all the faces of people he knew and also lots that he didn't. A lot of the women there were crying and all the men there looked really serious. His mum had kept calling him a brave soldier as they both walked to the front row of seats and sat beside a huge big brown box that sat on top of some shiny, metal stands.

'What's that?' Cian had asked his mum

'That's called a coffin and that's what your grandpa will use to get to heaven,' she answered

His mum had spoken about Grandpa going to this place called heaven for the last few days but he didn't know where it was. He knew the town he lived in, he knew the place where their caravan was, and he knew about a place called Egypt that his nursery school teacher had told him about, but he wasn't quite sure where heaven was.

'Is that the place in the sky mum?' he had asked, as he looked up at her in her black dress and big coat.

'That's right darling,' his mum had said, but she had then burst out crying and turned to cuddle his dad. Cian didn't ask any more about it.

It had been a very strange morning indeed. He had seen so many people but he hadn't seen his grandpa for a long time. The last time had been when he was sick in the hospital. Cian remembered that but he preferred to remember the times when he and grandpa had went fishing trips down the river; they had been much more fun.

Cian went through the hallway and asked some of the people if they had seen his grandpa, as he wanted to talk to him. Some of the men told him his grandpa was in heaven and his dad would tell him all about it. Some of the women had just started to cry and couldn't tell him anything. There were some really strange people at his house today.

'Cian,' whispered a voice behind him as he continued to walk along the hallway asking people where his grandpa was.

'Cian,' it whispered again behind him. But he was getting a little upset now as he went from person to person asking them about his grandpa but not getting any answers.

'Cian,' the voice whispered again, this time much closer.

'What?' shouted Cian as he spun round to look behind him.

There was no one there. There were people still standing at the sides of the hall but there was no one in the middle where the voice had been coming from.

'Come with me into the garden,' it whispered again.

Cian couldn't see where the voice was coming from but it sounded like it was right in front of him.

'Come on,' it said; this time sounding a bit further away at the back door to the garden. Cian shrugged and walked to the door. He didn't know who it was but the voice sounded really nice and soft; it was a bit like a mix between his dad's voice and his mum's voice.

'Over here,' said the voice coming from the bench in the garden

Cian walked over and sat on the bench looking at the big trees in the garden.

'Are you looking for your grandpa?' asked the voice. It sounded as if it was someone in the trees.

'Yes,' answered Cian, 'Who are you?' he asked

'I'm a Listener,' said the soft voice 'and I'll answer your questions.' Cian was happy to hear this. All he had wanted was for someone to listen to him and answer his questions.

'So where is my grandpa then?' Cian said, asking his first question

'Grandpa is in a place called heaven, which you've heard a lot of the adults telling you.' replied the voice. 'Heaven is an amazing place where people can go if they've been really sick or old and tired. Do you remember how sick your grandpa was in hospital?' said the voice

'Yes,' replied Cian, who could remember all the times that he saw his grandpa coughing and wheezing and struggling to breathe. He had looked in a lot of pain and it had upset Cian to see him that way.

'Well there's no sickness in heaven,' assured the voice, 'and your grandpa has went to a beautiful place where he is very happy and has lots of fun.'

'That sounds great,' said Cian happily, 'and is it up in the sky?' he asked

'That's right.' replied the voice

'Remember your little dog Joey went there last year and your mum told you how much better he would be feeling in heaven? Well it's the same place your grandpa is now, and not only is he happy but he's also able to play with Joey.' said the voice.

Cian had forgotten all about his little black dog Joey.

'That's right,' he said, 'Joey's little legs were very sore and he was always whimpering and then one day Mum told me he went to heaven where his legs would get better.'

'Exactly,' said the voice

'But I haven't seen Joey since he went away; will it be the same with Grandpa?' asked Cian

'Yes it will,' replied the voice, 'and you might get a bit sad from time to time when you can't see Grandpa but isn't it nice to know he's in a great place and feels so much better now and isn't in any pain?'

'It sure is,' said Cian very pleased with the thought, 'Is that why mum and dad have been crying? Because they can't see Grandpa anymore?' he asked

'Yes it is, and you'll have to help them understand how much better Grandpa is feeling now and how much fun you can still all have together as a family,' said the voice softly

'Can I go to heaven and see him?' asked Cian

'Not just now,' said the voice, when you're really old and tired then you can go to heaven and see him. There's so much to do where you are just now. Think of all the fun you have at nursery and with your friends and with your mum and dad.'

'Yeah, that's true. I'll stay here just now and see Grandpa later,' he said

'Good idea, there's loads of things to do,' said the voice 'and your Grandpa is able to watch you from heaven anyway and can see how much fun you're having and you can always talk to him

if you like because he will be able to hear you,'
continued the voice

Cian looked up to the fluffy clouds in the sky
and smiled 'Ah well, that's fine then,' he said
happily. 'But who are you again? Did you say a
Listener?' Cian asked

At that his mum shouted out of the back door,
'Cian, there you are. I was looking for you. Come
on in just now and say goodbye to Aunt Marie and
Uncle Jack' she said

'Ok,' shouted Cian and he jumped down from
the bench and ran happily into the house.

Tale 3 – New boy Connor

Erin was hanging her coat on the hook inside the hall at nursery when Cian walked in with his mum behind him.

'Hi Cian,' Erin said brightly, 'I haven't seen you for a while'

'Hi Erin,' he replied as he took off his coat. 'Yes, my Grandpa was really sick in hospital so I haven't been at school' he said.

'And is he better now?' she asked

'Yes he is,' Cian said brightly, 'He had to go to heaven to get all better and I won't be able to see him anymore until I'm really old and go to heaven too. But he's really happy and is having fun in heaven with little Joey.' he finished

'Oh well, that sounds great!' said Erin, 'Let's go into class' she offered

'Yes, let's go,' he said.

Cian turned to his mum who was smiling happily but her eyes seemed to be a little shiny and funny. He gave her a kiss and a hug and then ran into the class hand in hand with Erin.

The morning had been great. They had been painting pictures with Miss Dickie; they had played in the sand and water boxes; they had read a story in the reading corner; and they had a snack of apples and milk too. They had also met a new boy that the teacher had introduced as Connor who had just moved to the town with his mum and dad.

Connor seemed to be a nice boy and had helped make a great sand castle in the sand box but Tom had been naughty and had started to call Connor names while they were playing. Tom was always being naughty and not nice to the other boys and girls in nursery. Sometimes he would push boys over as they took their jackets off; sometimes he would pull the girls' pigtails and call them names. He could be quite a nuisance and was known as a bully. He would never share the toys; even when Erin had told him that her mum had said, 'sharing was caring'.

After morning snack, Miss Dickie rang the bell and all the children ran outside to play. They were all running about having a great time. Erin was skipping with some other girls and Cian was playing on the swings with some of the boys.

However, over in the corner near the big green bins, Tom was still being nasty to the new boy Connor. He was pushing him again and again and calling him 'smelly new boy'. Connor was not happy at this and asked him to stop but Tom just kept pushing and pushing.

Cian saw this from his swing and wasn't happy and wished that Tom would just play nice, but he wouldn't stop and none of the other children were saying anything. Cian wished and wished that Tom would stop bullying the new boy but he was afraid to say anything because Tom was bigger than him and had also pushed him around sometimes.

All the children kept playing and Tom kept being nasty to Connor. Cian was getting quite angry and wanted Tom to stop.

'Tell him to stop,' whispered a voice beside him

'You tell him, he's bigger than me,' said Cian as he turned to Paul who was playing on the swing beside him

'Eh?' said Paul confused, 'Tell who what?'

'It's me talking,' whispered the voice again, and Cian realised that it was The Listener talking.

'Where are you?' whispered back Cian

'I'm right with you,' it said, 'now tell Tom to stop bullying Connor'

'I can't. He's bigger than me.' Cian pleaded

'Yes you can,' said the voice softly, 'He's just a bully and all bullies are afraid. Tell him to stop and all the other children will help you.'

'But no-one else is telling him to stop' said Cian

'But it's not right what he's doing, is it?' asked the voice, 'And the other children will help you if you tell him to stop.' the voice assured him

'Hmm, I don't know,' mumbled Cian as he looked at how big Tom was. But the more that he saw Tom pushing Connor, Cian got really annoyed and wished it would stop. Just at that, Tom pushed Connor again and this time Connor fell over and hurt his knee on the paving stones and began to cry.

'That's it!' thought Cian, and he climbed out of his swing.

Just when he was about to shout, 'Stop it!' he heard someone else shout the words. It definitely wasn't Paul and it didn't sound like the Listener's soft voice either.

'Just stop it now you bully!' came the shout again.

It was Erin! And she was walking over to Tom from the spot where she had been skipping. Cian couldn't believe it.

'And what are you going to do about it?' sneered Tom at Erin. Tom stood up tall and lifted his fists as Erin approached him.

'I'm asking you to stop being a bully. And if you don't stop then I'll try and make you stop,' she said walking over

'Ha!' sneered Tom again, 'You're just a girl!'

'But I'm not,' said Cian as he started to walk from his swing towards Tom.

Cian looked over at Erin and winked; Erin smiled back. Tom got a bit startled as Cian walked towards him but began to smile a naughty smile again to pretend he wasn't bothered.

'And I'm not a girl either!' said a voice from behind Cian. Cian turned around to see that Paul was now also walking towards Tom.

'And we might be girls but we'll also stop you, you big bully!' cried two of the girls from behind Erin.

'And us,' said some of the other boys now from the slide.

Tom was looking quite scared now and his head quickly moved around as he saw all of the boys and girls walking towards him. He didn't look so big now and seemed to shrink down quite a bit. He took a step back but was right up against the wall and couldn't go any further. Tom was panicking now and he looked from side to side for an escape but there was none. Just as all the boys and girls were getting really close to him, Tom did something that none of the children had seen him do before.

He cried.

Tom fell to his knees, crying.

'Please don't hurt me,' squealed Tom and he hid his head in his hands.

The other children couldn't believe it. They had never seen him like this. He had always acted like a big tough bully but now that they were standing up to him, he just looked really scared.

'No one is going to hurt you,' said a voice from behind the crowd of children. They all looked round. It was the new boy Connor. He walked through the crowd, went right up to Tom and said again 'No one is going to hurt you.'

Tom peeked out from behind his hands, looking up at Connor who now stood right above him.

'No one likes a bully but if you play nicely like everyone else then everyone will like you and play with you,' assured Connor

'Is that right?' asked Tom, looking at all the other children that he had known for a long time but had never really got to know as friends. They all nodded back at him.

'Yes, that's right,' said Erin, 'we'd all like to play with you but we haven't been able to because you've always acted nasty and never shared your toys.'

Tom couldn't believe it. He had always acted tough and picked on the other boys and girls because he had thought that they just didn't like him. Now he understood that no one had played with him because he had always acted like a bully in the first place.

'Come on,' said Connor and he held out his hand, 'let's go kick the football to each other.'

Tom reached out and took Connor's hand. All the other children were smiling and started clapping. Connor pulled Tom up off his knees and they went over and played with the football on the little piece of grass just inside the school's gates.

'You were very brave to stand up to Tom there,' said Cian as he turned to Erin and smiled.

'Not really, I knew you would help me. The Listener told me,' she said.

Cian gasped, 'You know about The Listener?' he asked.

Just at that, the school bell rang and Miss Dickie came outside to call all the children into class.

Tale 4 – Lost in the woods

Erin's mum poured some orange juice into the Little Princess cup and placed it beside Erin's plate. It was Macaroni for dinner – Erin's favourite! She picked up her fork and began to devour her dinner hungrily, with little trickles of cheese sauce dribbling down her chin.

'Slow down,' said her mum

'But I need to hurry; Cian will be coming soon,' Erin muttered from her full mouth

'And no talking with your mouth full,' her mum interrupted, 'you know that's bad manners.'

Erin fell silent and continued to eat her dinner and drink her juice. She knew that Cian would be coming soon to play and the two of them could go out to the park. She loved going into the park; it seemed such a huge place. There was thick, dark green grass as far as the eye could see, and it was surrounded by gigantic trees that Cian and Erin would sometimes climb or hide behind.

The doorbell rang and Erin dropped her fork. Her mum stopped filling up the dishwasher and drew Erin a look.

'Yes, that'll be Cian but just you concentrate on finishing your dinner. You'll be going nowhere until you have an empty plate,' her mum said.

Erin's mum went to the door and sure enough, there was Cian and his mum.

'Hi Emma, come in. Hi Cian,' she said as she held back the front door.

Cian mumbled a quick hello and darted past her inside the house and through to the kitchen to see Erin. As the two mums sat down to a nice cup of tea in the living room, Cian and Erin talked in the kitchen about all the drawings they had made in Nursery that afternoon. Eventually, Erin finished her last fork full of Macaroni and put her plate up beside the sink.

'We want to go to the park!' shouted Erin and Cian together as they both ran into the living room.

'I wants, don't get!' replied their two mums at exactly the same time, and then looked at each other and burst out laughing.

'Please may we go to the park?' Erin started over again

'Yes you may,' said her mum, 'once you put your trainers on.'

Erin ran over to the couch and sat down on the floor beside her trainers. She peered inside one of them and seeing the letter 'R' scribbled in pen inside the trainer, she began to put it on her right foot. Her dad had made that mark on all of the right feet shoes, trainers, slippers and boots that Erin had, so that she would be able to put them on herself. Cian stood patiently and watched as Erin finished putting on both trainers. They then both shouted their farewells and ran towards the front door.

'Stop right there!' shouted Cian's mum and both kids stopped dead in their tracks and turned around.

'What things have you to remember?' she asked them

'Erm, not to cross the road,' started Cian

'To stay on the pavement outside the house and follow it round to the park,' continued Erin.

'Not to get mucky,' went on Cian

'And not to talk to any strangers.' finished Erin

'Except the Listener,' smiled Cian, 'but that's not a stranger.'

'Eh?' said his mum, 'Who?'

'Oh no-one,' he replied, 'we've not to talk to strangers,' he repeated and winked at Erin, who smiled back at him

'Right, ok then,' said his mum slowly eyeing the both of them, 'Just as well.' she finished

'Ok, off you go then and don't go far and I'll call on you to come back inside in 10mins,' added Erin's mum

'OK!' both kids shouted, and in a flash they had spun round, ran out the front door, slamming it behind them.

'What was that about a Listener?' Erin's mum asked Emma

'I don't know what they were on about,' Emma replied. 'Their imaginations run wild and those two are always up to something,' she chuckled. Both mums then went back to drinking their tea and talking about the exercise class they were going to go to on Tuesday night.

Meanwhile, outside, Erin and Cian were running down the pavement towards the park. It wasn't too far from their house but it always felt like a huge adventure. They ran side-by-side down the pavement. They jumped over the hole where the workmen had been digging beside the drain in the road. They waved as the big brown dog Mitch jumped up onto his wall and barked happily at them. Then they twisted round the corner that led them right into the big park. Both kids stopped and knelt down to feel the lovely long grass beneath them, then they ran on again right into the middle of the park and over to the trees.

They loved playing where the long line of trees stood at the edge of the park. There were always things to find there. In the autumn there would be big piles of crunchy leaves that they could run through. Sometimes they would find bits of paper or coins that had been accidentally dropped by people who walked their dogs along the line of trees. Cian loved looking for little ants and bugs that would be crawling over some of the big tree roots, and they had once come across a bird's nest that had fallen out of a tree after a day of really high winds.

From the edge of the park ran little paths that led into the trees and went away off into hidden alleys. Their mums had told them never to follow these paths and just play at the edge or in the park. Erin and Cian had made up stories about how the paths led to big castles or sleeping dragons.

They were passing the start of one of these paths when Cian suddenly stopped and held his hand against Erin to stop her walking also. Just when Erin was going to speak, Cian put a finger against his lips to silence her and pointed into the path. Erin turned her head and saw it. Right ahead of them, a little way along the path was a little baby bunny rabbit. They both looked at each other excitedly.

After standing still for several minutes and watching the little rabbit chew on a leaf, Cian started to slowly tiptoe onto the path and past the first tree. Erin gasped and reached out in silence, grabbing the back of his jumper.

'Stop, you can't go in there,' she whispered

'Just a little bit, so I can see the rabbit,' Cian whispered back and smiled.

Cian started to tiptoe along the path into the trees. He was holding his breath and trying to be as quiet as possible so that he didn't startle the little rabbit. Then all of a sudden three other little rabbits came out from behind a tree and joined the other rabbit eating some leaves.

Cian looked back at Erin who was still standing at the edge of the park. They were so excited but they both stayed silent. Cian waved an arm to invite Erin to follow him along the path.

All four little rabbits began to slowly hop away further along the path. Erin didn't want to miss seeing them so she started to quietly follow Cian along the path. Erin caught up with Cian as they took another turn along a different path following the rabbits as they all hopped along together.

'Look!' whispered Erin excitedly and pointing further up another path

'Wow!' whispered back Cian. There were dozens of other little rabbits all over the place. The woods were full of them. It was a beautiful scene with lots of little rabbits hopping around everywhere.

Cian and Erin slowly tiptoed along another path and round another corner as all the rabbits moved deeper and deeper into the woods. They were so busy following the rabbits that they hadn't noticed how far they had walked inside the woods far away from the park.

Cian lifted his left foot in the air to take another step along the path. 'Crack!' came the sound as Cian put his foot back down on the ground right on top of a twig.

Cian and Erin both stopped dead in their tracks. All of the rabbits had suddenly looked up at the sound and were now staring up at the children. Then it seemed like every single rabbit all vanished at once. They had hopped behind trees, ran down paths, jumped down holes, or snuck away through bushes. In a second they were gone and the children were left all alone.

'Oh, you scared them Cian!' moaned Erin

'I didn't mean to,' pleaded Cian, 'I stood on a twig by accident'

With all of the rabbits gone, the children shrugged their shoulders and turned around to walk back out to the park. They froze.

They now realised the park wasn't there. There were two paths in front of them, hundreds of trees and bushes, but no sign of the park.

They had walked deep into the woods and now had no idea what way they had come. Suddenly the trees seemed a lot bigger and darker than they had before. They could also hear lots of noises now that they hadn't noticed before; there were rustling, knocking and scratching noises. Both of them froze with fear, their little heads quickly looking all around them, trying to remember which way they had come.

'Cian, I'm scared,' whispered Erin

'I'm a little scared too, but we'll be ok,' replied Cian

'How are we going to get back out? It's already starting to get a little dark,' appealed Erin

'I'm not sure but if we calm down we should be able to find our way out,' said Cian. 'I think.' he added uncertainly

Both Cian and Erin looked ahead at the two paths that lay in front of them. They had no idea which one they had walked down but they started to stare at them, hoping they'd see something that they remembered, but both paths looked exactly the same. As they stood silently staring, their breathing started to slow down. Then a voice whispered from in front of them.

'That's it,' it said, 'calm down and look at the paths'

'The Listener!' the children shouted together

'What, can you hear him too?' asked Cian turning to Erin

'Him? The Listener is a girl,' replied Erin

'No he's not. It's a boy and he speaks to me,' insisted Cian

'I think you'll find she's a girl. It's obviously a girl's voice and she helps me!' retorted Erin

'I actually talk to both of you,' interrupted the voice, 'and I sound like a boy to Cian and a girl to Erin, so you're both right. Now shall we all get back to the park?' the Listener asked

'Yes please,' both children replied

'Ok then,' said the voice, 'you both know how this works by now. You have to start with making sure your breathing is really deep and slow.'

Both Cian and Erin started to breathe a lot slower. They both held their hands on their tummies, feeling for the air filling up, and they stared forward at the paths in front of them.

'That's it,' said the voice pleased with the both of them. 'Now I want you to keep breathing and keep looking at the paths. They both look the same to you just now but keep looking. Keep looking for beauty, one of the pathways will look more beautiful than the other,' the voice finished saying.

Both children stood silently and breathing deeply. Both paths looked exactly the same with the trees and bushes around them looking just the same colour and height. The stones on the path were the same colour, and the paths were the same size.

Then, Erin started to notice a small clump of yellow flowers beside the path on the left. Without saying a word, Cian's eyes also started to notice the flowers. He hadn't spotted them before but there they were, a tiny little bunch of yellow flowers and the more he kept looking, the brighter they seemed to get. The flowers were also looking brighter to Erin; it was as if the yellow was getting deeper and brighter and the more she kept looking, the more the flowers stood out.

'The flowers,' whispered Erin

'Yes, the yellow ones at the left path,' whispered back Cian

'That's right,' said the voice, 'the path you should choose is the one on the left. The beauty in nature will always show you the correct way to go.'

'Thanks for helping us again Listener,' said Erin, 'but...who are you?'

'Yes, who are you? And will you always be able to help us?' asked Cian

There was total silence for a few seconds then the mysterious voice began to talk softly again; it sounded as if it was coming from the trees right in front of them.

'Yes, I will always be here for you,' it said, 'I am a Listener and I will always be able to help you because I am deep inside you.'

Both children looked at each other startled. The voice continued,

'I have always been able to help you and you're able to hear me in different voices because I am in your hearts; I *am* your hearts.

'You never need to be afraid of anything you face in your lives. Anytime that you're not sure what path you should take, anytime you're afraid of something or just don't know what to do, I'll be here to listen and guide you. You won't be able to hear my voice again after this but you'll be able to *feel* my answers.

'Whatever question you have, just slow down your breathing as I've taught you and put the question deep into your hearts. Picture it there and wait. You'll eventually be able to feel me guiding you and you'll know what to do. As you grow older you'll forget about me ever talking to you but if you ask your questions in the way I've shown you, I'll always be here to listen and guide you. Do you understand?'

Both children nodded and said, 'Yes, thank you.'

As they stood there, the children couldn't hear the voice talking anymore but they weren't afraid. All of the noises around them didn't scare them now either, they sounded interesting and nice. The trees looked tall and beautiful, not dark and scary. They could now see and hear lots of little animals; birds in the trees and little mice and squirrels scurrying around the ground in the woods.

Cian held out his hand and Erin took it in hers. They both smiled huge smiles and looked at each other. They knew they would never be afraid of anything ever again.

They turned towards the left path and hand in hand they ran happily out of the woods, back to the park, and back to their mums.

Printed in the United Kingdom by
Lightning Source UK Ltd., Milton Keynes
138868UK00001B/30/P